DEMOCRACY

BY M. WEBER

Published by The Child's World®
1980 Lookout Drive • Mankato, MN 56003-1705
800-599-READ • www.childsworld.com

PHOTO CREDITS
Ariel Skelley/Getty Images, cover, 2; Tetra images RF/Getty
Images, 5; Hulton Archive/Getty Images, 6, 11; Wellcome Library,
London/Wellcome Images/Wikimedia, 6; Godfrey Kneller/
Wikimedia, 9; United States Architect of the Capitol/John
Trumbull/Wikimedia, 12; Publius/Wikimedia, 14; Mr. Matté/
Wikimedia, 17; The New York Times/Wikimedia, 19; Speaker.gov/
Wikimedia, 20

ISBN 9781503844995 (REINFORCED LIBRARY BINDING)
ISBN 9781503846333 (PORTABLE DOCUMENT FORMAT)
ISBN 9781503847521 (ONLINE MULTI-USER EBOOK)
LCCN 2019956647

Printed in the United States of America

On the cover: Voting is one of the most
important parts of a democracy.

TABLE OF CONTENTS

CHAPTER 1

History of Democracy...4

CHAPTER 2

The Beginning of Democracy in America...10

CHAPTER 3

American Democracy Today...16

GLOSSARY...22

TO LEARN MORE...23

INDEX...24

ABOUT THE AUTHOR...24

HISTORY OF DEMOCRACY

There are many forms of government. Some governments give power to a king or queen. Other governments share power with citizens. Citizens are people who live in a country, state, or city. The word "democracy" means "rule by the people." That means people have power. They help choose their leaders. These leaders are called politicians. Politicians work as **representatives** in government. People vote in a democracy. They vote in **elections**. The voice of the people is very important. They vote on new laws. They vote for people to represent them in government. Some representatives work for a long time. Sometimes, voters choose someone new. This is all part of how democracy works.

Democracy has a long history. It started in ancient Greece. Two **philosophers** helped create the idea. Plato and Socrates lived around 400 BC. They debated many important ideas.

Voting is one of the most important parts of democracy.

Plato

Socrates

That means they discussed what made ideas good or bad. One of those ideas was democracy. It was a new form of government. They talked about how democracy could work. They saw some problems from the beginning. Democracy needs people to make good choices. People need information. Then they can make good choices. But it still seemed like a good idea. Athens, Greece, was ruled by a democratic government. It was the first official democracy. Some of those ideas are still used today. For example, democracy always includes voting. Other ideas have changed. For example, only men who finished military training could vote in ancient Greece.

There are two main types of democracy. One is direct democracy. The government in Athens was a direct democracy. That means every citizen votes on every decision. In Athens, voters gathered together in one place. They gathered in the main square of the city. Then they voted together on major issues.

There is also representative democracy. This means people choose representatives. Representatives speak for the people. They gather to vote on major issues. Citizens can tell their representatives what they want. However, the politician gets to decide how to vote. A country with a representative democracy is also called a **republic**. Most democracies today are representative. Other philosophers have added to the idea of democracy. John Locke called democracy the "rule of the **majority**." That means the largest group of people set the rules.

Democracy has changed since ancient Greece. But some things are the same. Democratic governments all share similar requirements. First is citizens rule. Power cannot be taken away from citizens. The second requirement is free elections. A free election means the government cannot stop anyone from voting. Citizens do not need to tell anyone who they voted for. Third is protecting all rights. Democracy is based on majority opinion. But the majority cannot vote away the rights of a **minority** group. Finally, citizens are urged to vote! They also need to learn about issues. Citizens need to know their representatives. This helps democracy work.

John Locke inspired the men who created America's first government. Thomas Jefferson even used some of Locke's ideas while writing the Declaration of Independence.

CHAPTER 2

THE BEGINNING OF DEMOCRACY IN AMERICA

Democracy has a long history in the United States. The US was founded on July 4, 1776. The American **colonies** declared independence from Great Britain. Early America was made up of colonies. The colonies were ruled by Great Britain. They did not have a voice. The king of Great Britain made choices for them. The people wanted to make their own choices. America decided to form a democracy. It was the first country to start off as a democracy.

Starting a new country was not easy. Great Britain did not want to give up control. But the colonists wanted to be independent. They thought the British king treated them unfairly. They disagreed on many issues.

AMERICA'S FIRST ELECTION

The first presidential election in America took place on January 7, 1789. George Washington ran for president. He had led the army during the Revolutionary War (1775–1783). The candidate with the second-most votes was John Adams. He became vice president.

Before America had its own government, its citizens
had to follow the laws of Great Britain.

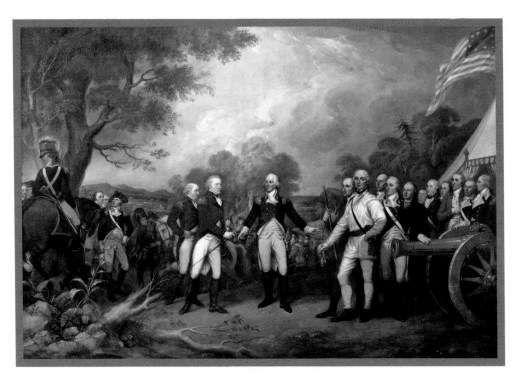

General George Washington led the American colonies to freedom from British rule.

One of those issues was **taxes**. Americans paid taxes to the king. However, he did not take care of the colonies. The colonists had to fight a war against the British. It was called the Revolutionary War. America won the Revolutionary War. The citizens were ready to choose their own leaders.

Many people helped create the United States. Some of these people are called the Founding Fathers. The Founding Fathers did many things. They talked about issues. They wrote important documents. These documents helped build the new government.

One of these documents is called the Constitution. The Constitution is the highest law in the United States. All other laws are based on the Constitution.

The Constitution also created branches of government. There are three branches. The first is the executive branch. It carries out the laws. The president is the head of this branch. The second is the legislative branch. It makes the laws. Citizens elect representatives to **Congress**. Congress is the legislative branch. The third branch is the judicial branch. It makes sure everyone follows the law. The judicial branch is made up of all the courts and judges. Citizens go to court when they break the law.

The Constitution also created important rules. They are still in place today. One is called "separation of powers." This means that all three branches of government are equal. In Great Britain, the king was more powerful than anyone else. But in the United States, the president shares power in government. The Constitution created federalism. That means the federal government controls the whole country. Federalism splits power between the federal government and the states. All states must follow the Constitution. However, they can also make their own laws.

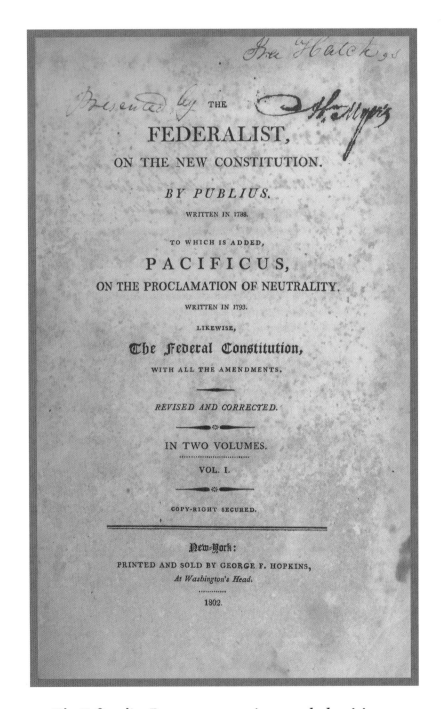

The Federalist Papers were written to help citizens understand the new laws in the US Constitution.

The Founding Fathers made many decisions. They chose to be a representative democracy. The states had to agree with their decisions. Some of the Founding Fathers wrote essays. These essays are called *The Federalist Papers*. *The Federalist Papers* explained the Constitution. All of the states had to vote on the Constitution. Two-thirds of the states had to agree on it. The Constitution became the law in 1788. This is considered the official start of democracy in the United States.

George Washington was the first president of the United States. He served for two terms. A presidential term is four years. John Adams was elected as the second president. Washington had to agree to leave office. He gave the power to John Adams. This is called the peaceful transfer of power. It is one of the most important parts of democracy. Democracy means that no one can lead forever. The people choose a new president every four years. Washington gave a speech when he left office. The speech is still remembered today. It praised the peaceful transfer of power.

CHAPTER 3

AMERICAN DEMOCRACY TODAY

The United States has been a democracy for more than 200 years. It is one of the oldest democracies in the world. Many parts of the government have changed. But some things have stayed the same. The government was split into different levels from the beginning. The three levels are federal, state, and local. The federal level controls the whole country. These laws apply to everyone. State laws only apply to citizens in a certain state. The local level is even smaller. Examples of local government include cities and counties. Citizens have many representatives.

WAITING FOR APPROVAL

Not every **amendment** to the Constitution has passed. The Equal Rights Amendment was proposed in 1971. It promised equal rights for women. However, only 34 states ratified the Equal Rights Amendment. It needed the approval of 38 states to become law.

Based on its population, New Jersey has 12
members in the House of Representatives.

City council members represent the people in a city government. State senators represent all the people who live in a state. They work for that state's government. The president represents all of the country's citizens.

Sometimes, the government wants to make big changes. That means they must change, or amend, the Constitution. The Constitution had 10 amendments at first. They are called the Bill of Rights. Seventeen other amendments have also been added to the Constitution. There are now 27 total. States have to agree to add an amendment. This is called ratification. At least two-thirds of the states must agree. That means 38 of the 50 states have to agree. Amendments to the Constitution are meant to make the United States better. For example, the 13th Amendment ended slavery.

The United States has changed since 1776. Rules about democracy have also changed. Not everyone could vote at first. Only white men who owned land were allowed to vote. Many people were left out of elections. Women could not vote. African Americans could not vote. This was unfair. People began to speak out. First, white men who did not own land were given voting rights. Then the 15th Amendment was passed. It came after the Civil War.

Suffragists organized parades in New York and Washington, DC, to campaign for voting rights for all US citizens.

The 15th Amendment said men of every race could vote. But women still could not vote. Women wanted the law changed to allow them to vote. The women's **suffrage** movement started in 1848. It called for voting rights for all people. It took more than 70 years. The 19th Amendment was finally passed in 1920. This amendment gave women the right to vote.

There are 535 members of Congress. They include
US senators and the House of Representatives.

The US government represents the people. All people
want to be treated fairly. The US government takes a census
every 10 years. This is an official count of all the people in
the country. The Constitution requires the government to
do this. The government uses the information it collects. It
tells the government how many representatives each state
gets. It also helps to make different **districts**.

Districts should be the same size. This is how people are represented fairly. Big cities are often split into many districts. Smaller towns might just have one.

US citizens are represented in Congress. Congress makes laws. The House of Representatives is one part of Congress. Representatives are sent based on a state's population. Population is the number of people who live in a state. Small states like Delaware have only one representative. States with more people have many. California has 53.

The Senate is the second part of Congress. Every state gets two senators. It doesn't matter if the state's population is big or small. People also vote for president. Votes are counted through the **Electoral College** in a presidential election. Each state's electoral votes are based on population. One **candidate** wins the majority of the votes in a state. That candidate wins all the electoral votes.

American democracy continues to be important today. Other countries want to see how democracy works. US citizens are always working to make it better. Elections happen every year. The government is always changing. This is because democracy is about the power of the people.

amendment (uh-MEND-munt) An amendment is a change in the words or meaning of a law or document, such as a constitution.

archaeologists (ar-kee-AH-luh-jists) Archaeologists are scientists who study past human life and activities by studying the bones, tools, etc., of ancient people.

candidate (KAN-di-det) A candidate is a person who runs for offices.

colonies (KOL-uh-neez) Colonies are areas of one country that are owned and governed by another country.

congress (KON-gris) A congress is a formal meeting in which representatives or experts discuss important matters and make decisions for a government.

districts (DIS-trikts) Districts are areas established by a government for official government business.

elections (el-EK-shunz) Elections are processes of choosing someone for a public office by voting.

Electoral College (i-LEK-ter-ul KAL-lej) The Electoral College the process by which someone is elected president. It is made up of 538 representatives from all 50 states. To be elected president, a candidate must receive 270 electoral votes.

majority (muh-JOR-i-tee) The majority is the largest number of people or votes.

minority (my-NOR-i-tee) The minority is the smaller number of a group of people, usually less than half.

philosophers (fil-AH-si-ferz) Philosophers are people who study ideas about knowledge, truth, and the nature and meaning of life.

representatives (rep-ri-ZEN-tuh-tivz) Representatives are people who are chosen in elections to act or speak for the people who voted for them.

republic (ree-PUB-lik) A republic is a country that is governed by elected representatives and by an elected leader, such as a president, rather than by a king or queen.

suffrage (SUF-rij) Suffrage is the right to vote in an election.

taxes (TAKS-iz) Taxes make up an amount of money that a government requires people to pay according to their income, the value of their property, etc. The government uses taxes to pay for programs, such as building roads.

IN THE LIBRARY

Bonwill, Ann. *We Can Vote*. New York, NY: Children's Press, 2019.

Mooney, Carlia. *The U.S. Constitution: Discover How Democracy Works*. White River Junction, VT: Nomad Press, 2016.

Shamir, Ruby. *What's the Big Deal About Elections*. New York, NY: Philomel Books, 2018.

ON THE WEB

Visit our website for links to learn more about democracy:

childsworld.com/links

Note to Parents, Teachers, and Librarians: We routinely verify our Web links to make sure they are safe and active sites. So encourage your readers to check them out!

INDEX

Bill of Rights, 18

Congress, 13, 20, 21
Constitution, 13, 14, 15, 16, 18, 20

direct democracy, 7
districts, 20, 21

elections, 4, 8, 10, 18, 21, 22
Electoral College, 21

The Federalist Papers, 14, 15

Great Britain (British), 10, 11, 12, 13

Locke, John, 8, 9

majority, 8, 21
minority, 8

Plato, 4, 6

representative democracy, 8, 15
representatives, 4, 8, 13, 16, 20, 21
republic, 8
Revolutionary War, 10, 12

Socrates, 4, 6
suffrage, 19

taxes, 12

Washington, George, 10, 12, 15

ABOUT THE AUTHOR

M. Weber is a teacher and writer. She has written for both kids and adults and enjoys helping people of all ages learn new things. She has written about history, sports, and the environment. When she is not writing, she enjoys spending time with her family and browsing at her local bookstore. She lives in Minnesota.